Kimono Mountain

Mike Parker

ECO/CO Books
Middle Creek Publishing
Beulah, CO. USA

Kimono Mountain Poems
© 2017, Mike Parker

No part of this book may be reproduced by any means known at this time or derived henceforth without written permission of the publisher or author. The exception would be in the case of brief quotations embodied in the critical articles or reviews and pages where permission is specifically granted by the publisher or author.

Books may be purchased in quantity and/or special sales by contacting the publisher. All inquiries related to such matters should be addressed to:

Middle Creek Publishing & Audio
9027 Cascade Avenue
Beulah, CO 81023
editor@middlecreekpublishing.com
(719) 369-9050

Cover Design: David A. Martin, Middle Creek Publishing
Printed in the United States
Author Photo: Courtesy of Lauren Hereford

First Edition, 2017

ISBN: 978-0-9989322-3-1

Kimono Mountain Poems
Mike Parker
1. Human Ecology   2. Poetry   3. Colorado

For

Emily Armstrong & Pat Ivers
Cindy Dellorfano & Anthony Varrone
Mary & Frannie
Inspirational friends
Peter Dougherty
Anita Sarko
Alan Vega

Contents

11	The Time is Ripe
12	Lineage
13	Dec. 7 2016
14	Sometimes He Liked t' Frame His Own
15	Fossils
16	Coming Apart
17	Vampire Cosmetics at Rocky Flats
20	She Blushes
21	Trimming
22	11-9 9-11 11-9 9-11
23	The Runoff
24	August 25 The Daily Difficult
25	Casualty
26	Ali
28	Old MSR Snowshoes
29	Jan 20
30	Unsteady
31	August 27 Aspens Tremble
32	Practice Buoyancy
33	Existential Bliss
34	Orlando Slaughter
35	Joan o' Spark
36	Elegy
37	March 2 Somewhere Else
38	Kimono Mountain
39	Jan 30, 2017
40	Oct 27 Bald Head
41	Fall Fell

42	March 16 The Poor Just Paving Stones
43	Sept 26, 2016 Stalker
44	April 13 Developing Storm
45	July 9 Wild Roses
46	March 7 Crawling Intent
47	Nov 24 No Abode
48	Dancing with Friends
49	Spring Melt
50	How to Make Your Own Kimono
54	Night Meal
55	OxyMoron in the White House
56	Parkerganda
57	August Hail

Kimono Mountain

Poems

Mike Parker

The Time is Ripe

eat the fruit of your labors
treason is in season
serve big helpings of refusals
(rich get richer
poor almost get paid)

Mike Parker

Lineage

father was a snow shovel
mother a handful of kindling
i was the last wooden match
in the box

Kimono Mountain

Dec. 7 2016

polar vortex cold kiss
-20° snow every day
wind hiss winter's near miss
now rides december's remember
shovel tired
nightfires admire cast iron
icy dendrites on single panes
weather as prevalent art form
storm after storm piled high
nightsky veiled moon sighs

Mike Parker

Sometimes He Liked t' Frame His Own
    for Jeff Freund

Jean-Michel Basquiat, 1981
the new Picasso
unconscious taxi backseat
O.D. side of nightclub Tier 3

been humping death all day
hypodermic embroidered arms
self-harm alarms anoint
growing fame's spiky charm

strapped down puking
a paint spattered kid
about t' kiss a stomach pump
emergency room St. Vincent's

threw him over a shoulder
so he could do it again
saw him next night
glassy eyed rope a dope
in a fight with himself
a contender looking for a draw

Kimono Mountain

Fossils

I hold   cherish   corpses
a once living trail 2 billion years
remnants of extinctions
reclaimed by minerals the breathing
long gone- the planet a casket
cratered by intruders
pockmarking geo eras
celestial tattoo splattering
whole species vaporized
the stuff of crawled & oozed
now in my hands history snoozed

Mike Parker

Coming Apart

raven warnings
hover over spilled seed
noisy promises greed the fear
of the coming year coming apart-
he's the ultimate bad landlord
on the phone- your lease is up
raising the rent
turning down the heat
his vice new super with fangs
gentrified genocide
global swarming riptide millionaires
goldmansacking our affordable

Kimono Mountain

Vampire Cosmetics at Rocky Flats
    (for Roy Young, Daniel Ellsberg, Allen Ginsberg,
     the Truth Force protesters and their allies in waging peace)

-1957 Unreported massive fire in building 771 bathing Boulder Broomfield Arvada and Denver in plutonium and toxic contamination
-thousands of steel drums leaking thru 1960's downsoil into Woman Creek and into Standley Lake Reservoir
-thousands of pondcrete boxes containing waste oil tools gloves filters tainted by plutonium- it won't set solid and sits leaking
-1989 FBI raids Rocky Flats collecting evidence and testimony from workers about environmental fraud and dangerous working conditions. Oddly in 1994 the Rocky Flats Nuclear Weapons Plant is renamed the Rocky Flats Environmental Technology Site
-2000 U.S. Fish and Game signs into law the Rocky Flats National Wildlife Refuge
-2004 U.S. Fish and Wildlife Service announces its public recreation plan for the 4000 acre site outside the still deadly legacy site of 2000 acres behind signs & fences

    vampire cosmetics
    cleanup was a coverup
    americium cesium tritium plutonium
    nature's deep gash
    desecrated for weapons & cash
    now they're ready t' breach the dam

Mike Parker

across Woman Creek
let the poisoned sediment flow
dry & blow give Broomfield deadly rash
the flood of 2013 moved
americium cesium tritium plutonium

muddy slopes sliding downstream
bad dream forest service peddling
recreational curses with glowing nurses
hike hunt bike jog embalm
plutonium 24,000 year timethrob
rob your bloodstream
lustdust recreates this funeral parlor
release taste disgrace into thyroids
nightmare leukemic trout in uranium butter
shudder in deadly chinook winds
americium cesium tritium plutonium
prairie dogs burrowing up deadly soil
will poison raptors will poison coyote
foxes skunk black bear hot deer
stir up horrible past
new neighborhoods breathing it in
it sits on one of the windiest
corridors in the west- it tumbles
trailers trucks- what of innocent lungs?
U.S. Fish & Game Management pushing
propaganda coffin containing demolished resolutions
all those leaking steel barrels
embalming the water table 40 years

Kimono Mountain

inspectors disabled under the table
ghosts of doomed workers hot lungs
unreported accidents & fires
reborn in downwind duststorms
shoddy new real estate with open windows
kids toys digging in front lawns
americium cesium tritium plutonium
rodents with terrible fevers

mountain bikes pedaled by skeletons
raptors falling featherless
open space contagious contaminants
don't let it happen again
react react react
vampire cosmetics
cleanup was a coverup
no altering permanent facts
americium cesium tritium plutonium

Mike Parker

She Blushes

after laying there
all winter under rumpled
covers she finally
pokes her head out & blushes –
spring rhubarb

Kimono Mountain

Trimming

bud mounds piled high
scissors manicure little leaves
red hairs sticky promises
flipped into the bag-
pounds t' go trim
turn the flower trim it
vapors vamp noses
bag filling sticky hands
turn & trim trim trim
trim trim trim
j's passing smoky halo
bag filling we three chilling
trim & turn trim trim
dump another harvest
lavender sativa maui indica
hands covered in crystals
scissors singing trim trim
clippings dunked in snowwater
THC congeals and balls up in net
bubble hash squeezed from debris

Mike Parker

11-9 9-11 11-9 9-11

devastation   the bomb went off
guard your daughters from vengeance
supreme court fashion nooses
instead of robes- peace of mind attacked
segregation sexism open season on immigrants
foreign policy rears ugly head
civil liberties atomic drones Trump tattooed
on our daughters' hopes
white women voted for a molester
sequester the promise of a free semester
talk with your sons talk t' your sons
prepare t' fight the bully pulpit
open your heart t' each other
refuse t' let white smother color
the bomb in the booth went off
fallout Assad and Putin cheer results
their destination is devastation
guard your daughters stay healthy
you're no longer covered
organize your close ties
discover new strengths
find hope in your neighbor
find hope in each other
find hope find hope find hope

Kimono Mountain

The Runoff

tends his red tulips
torching his green yard
endless rains lame refrain
time's burden bends him
the weight of knowing
chemo is over
no experimental meds left
he's unloading his books
but still planting clones
along his path sweet peas
sulphur flowers and bluebells
adorn the runoff
                the runoff

Mike Parker

August 25   The Daily Difficult

latesummer cold rains
radio lame with emails
& racist walls
it's decency's last call
before they turn off the light-
the daily difficult
trying t' make ends meet
greets us w/ a choice
voice it
defeat or defiance
interdependent self-reliance
instead of their threatening finance
oh t' be
    more than a deductible

Kimono Mountain

Casualty

black bears awake
a month early

first robins worming

mountain lion stalks
cold spring road
mourning creekside
its carslain child

carcass lay there
two days on the curve
serenaded by ravens
halo of praying flies

Mike Parker

Ali

Muhammed & me   we
were recently both hospitalized
they thought we were both
about t' die in bed
he did   i didn't
almost still breaths
once again i escaped
my genetics   -but someday!

tonite i remember his kindness
bailing out the convalescent home
in Brooklyn with boxing savings-

his confidence his halo
a brash hello in a world
now looking down at tweets-
his fist always more open than closed

America divided over Viet Nam
it was 1968 on the corner
East 6th Street & Avenue A
in a terrible downpour
on my way t' the corner bodega
waiting for the light t' change-
heard the poolroom door open
behind me people laughing-
i couldn't stop sneezing
felt a big hand on my shoulder

Kimono Mountain

turned & looked up t' him-
"little brother get outta the rain
take care of yourself"
a moment hard t' believe
said "i'm a C.O. too
i'm not going either"
he patted my shoulder
laughing "little brother take care"
got in a cab- New York moment

back home soaked
bagful of courage
refused t' kill for them
they took his title away
threatened me with prison
hell no we didn't go

tonite still breathing
feeling that hand
on my shoulder
alive or dead
still that rainy taste
courage in my mouth
wouldn't shut up
not then   not now

Mike Parker

Old MSR Snowshoes

north on the Sourdough trail
mind glides in someone's
ski tracks   it's windless

old MSR snowshoes
best friends
700 miles on them
cross frozen lakes
thru blowing drifts
devouring miles bred smiles
St. Vrain creek beneath March ice
Canada jay joins in
singingcreek forest chorus
full of ripe intentions

Kimono Mountain

Jan 20

snow veils January gray
nothing more t' say
thoughts turned t' hay

Mike Parker

Unsteady

hearing lost sight unsteady
every day habitual ritual
a walker instead of spouse's arm
to hold on to the time left
complaints about the food
life savings leaking
hope leaking unsteady
everything leaking
making the best of it
the worst of it the daily
habitual rituals numb commiserate
the time left unsteady
communities mostly women
men buried years ago unsteady
i'm thankful for my axe & shovel
family & snowshoes & a way t' pay the bills

Kimono Mountain

August 27   Aspens Tremble

banjo breeze
high strung
bubble hashed
thunder heads moan
hyacinths pink the
high grass no need
t' water
still wet & green
fall chores can't ignore
decreosote stovepipes
sit   adjust thermostat
place i'm at
mind accordion's
counting breaths-
jets head for ISIS
Ebola & Zika quarantines
bleach blessed
geography anointed
aspens tremble

Mike Parker

Practice Buoyancy

> *"And the burden*
> *that you carry*
> *turns to light"*
> *-Reed Bye*

buddhist country song
imagination blizzards path
bootprints in the void-
sound of one mouth
laughing-   pumped up flat tireds
accidental meetings around corners
cashmering my ears

Kimono Mountain

Existential Bliss

i see shooting stars
flock of ironnickel rocks
flying this way
mocking the odds
don't say never
a change in the interest rate
won't help this stress test
evolve didn't mean solve

Mike Parker

Orlando Slaughter

49 dead in a dance bar
Trump vomits macho disease
Brazil is under house arrest
Olympians breaststroke thru swill
sales of automatics swell
homeless hole in America's shoe
our fates are limping limping
disco gunfires a funeral tattoo-
shut off lunchbreak NPR
back t' my chopping block
brief respite in chores t' do
i know they'll never manhandle
the laws in the flaws of science
it's been a heavy week
but neutron stars weigh a billion tons
per teaspoon
black holes weigh more than
a million of our suns-
broadcast black eyes abuse a bluebird day

Kimono Mountain

Joan o' Spark

Coldsprings fire almost contained
houses gone lives in cinders
Ward radio update lifeline
wind's blowing this way?
our crews hacking a line
mercury soaring planes bombing
red gush suppressed
Pam Harrington rides thru the flames
like some Joan of Spark
defending trapped horses

Mike Parker

Elegy
   (Gene Parker)

his strength his family
his marriage his glory
he was a lilting Irish story
from Washington Hill t' Kerry
dignity and hope his railings
his friends his trophies
lonelier life without you
but memories thatched tight
against the rains of time
my brother my friend
'till we meet again

Kimono Mountain

March 2   Somewhere Else

my eaves are dripping
first bear in Boulder busted
bailed out w/ a tag a net a ride
somewhere else
my metal roof slides its thud
spring melt waterboards predictable
lies! lies!
the truth has a sty

Mike Parker

Kimono Mountain

Kimono Mountain
is that place
inside our tides
to sit in a windbreak-
give up what's at stake
breath & slowly bag it
let embers glow
nothing t' no

Kimono Mountain

Jan 30, 2017

cowering airports   customs terrorize
refugees & demand green cards
the no-fly can't stay list swells
like a bad bruise's bad news
in Quebec prayer rugs soaked in blood
the snipers in Mosul crosshair a soccergame
Bannon as Goebbels rebirth makes a list
this is the sound of January goosestepping
handcuffs windchime a tornado of fear

Mike Parker

Oct 27   Bald Head

a front kick t' the spleen
all the sit-ups in the universe
all the knowing inevitable
all the samsara insight
even the end of your pain
nothing prepared me
for the knock on my door
nothing eased a friend no more
last words
   "go for a long walk
   don't come by i'm gone
   kiss my bald head
   i'm outta here"
i balk- "beat it sucker
   don't cancel reading for me"
last wave
      too hard to talk

Kimono Mountain

Fall Fell

last butterflies
shoot the breeze
pollen hunting

buttercups full o' flies
ants moving ants
reds & greens
browns & tans
demand eyes relax

Lake Isabelle moose meander
rest in shady poolside
chew willows & waddle
their unsaddled pride
at being alive late September
can't remember
a more colorful year

Mike Parker

March 16   The Poor Just Paving Stones

punches predict strategy
promises mouthed statistically
superdelegates steal the show
established superpacs wait & drool
fear unites fear ignites
the poor just paving stones t' throw
the winner will kill & drill
threaten & drone- the unemployed
will lose a home chew old bones
super tuesdays spread their virus-
up here light snow
no pundits pandering prime time
Asian doves welcome the sun
low pressure building
local kids voice Ward radio
robins are back
little shacks shelter our backs

Kimono Mountain

Sept 26, 2016   Stalker

high pitched screaming
awakens daughter's sleep
moonlit cold night screaming-
morning half a rabbit
walking thru bloodstained
on my way t' hitch t' work-
cougar done its shift
picking a bone with hunger

Mike Parker

April 13   Developing Storm

flickas' singing
johnny jump-ups eye poppin'
colors hopping
tulips! daffodils! can't stop 'em
fog falling temp dropping
upslope heavy wet & white tonite
spring in the Rockies
mindhockey radio news
dampfuse beneath m' muse

Kimono Mountain

July 9   Wild Roses

behind outhouse
young flies
have a quorum
in the wild roses
voting on
the summer's perfume-
scatter when i move
even a fly
can feel my
intentions

Mike Parker

March 7   Crawling Intent

flock of orange robins
red pine grosbeaks twin
magpies   blue stellar jays
chickadees in heat
juncos pecking snowy sunflower
seeds
   the neighbor's cat beside herself
stalking crawling low   intent
mindbent   first redwing blackbirds

Kimono Mountain

Nov 24   No Abode

sunny face
porch scorch
well squandered
November blue
thinking 'bout you
moving thru
middle bardos
light at the end
of the funnel
keep moving
atoms pave
perishable possible
you're in eternity
no worries
been there before
no abode
just a door

Mike Parker

Dec 29   Dancing with Friends

ending year's doubts
politicians' promise continued
violence- endless drones
ISIS crisis, moaning refugees
holding infants, razorwire borders
terminal terror hisses hopeless
two-legged mammal mess
police incidents on dashboard
twitters-
the harvest have-nots seem t' never
nude selfies extracurricular servers
hands once replaced by
faces looking down at devices
hey! where your app?
look up!
hope in my daughter's eyes
extra blanket in wife's smile
hours spent with co-workers mend
constant chopping & shoveling strengthen
decency is dancing with friends
blessings as soups made & eaten
balance must be practiced
or we all fall
doubt is a ball
that must be chewed
virtual virtue pays its dues
look up or down
you choose

Kimono Mountain

Spring Melt

new green pushing midday
thunderheads echo
continental divide

radio primary results
mob t' lynch decency
insult
      thieves
guilty of the people's
wantings
they offer us
minimum rage
try & spend that at Whole Foods

but the daffodils
throaty yellow
chorus above radio blues
tells my shovel t' relax
big blizzards over
slow meltings gift
pasque flowers
bust thru drifts

Mike Parker

How to Make Your Own Kimono

i wanted what i had

upslope the maples hickory oak & ginseng
peridot damp mosses springs trickling
watercolor scarves foggy around
the necks of hemlocks
above west chestnut creek-
i climbed Kimono connecting
brown dot blotter entrances
bluestone caves & woodcuts sageing
the unpaved mountain mystics path
digging ginseng waistdeep in stinging
nettles upslope in paradise
in the arms of Kimono mountain
tucked deep in traver hollow catskills
a love affair everyday
just walking out the door
of a roughcut cabin we shared
retreating from cities   a softness
without media's vomit
meandering in soft rains
Kimono's silky smooth healed us
deer paths thru white birch
banqueted the vision we had
of our future- we were
on a mission t' go nowhere now
t' climb Kimono daily taught us
the way t' erase-

Kimono Mountain

i'll never forget the first time
i watched the breeze undress her
soaked in gray mist-
you undid the sash of August
it dropped off your shoulders
& i wanted what i had

inking the fabric is done
with cold pressed botanicals
steeped for winters on woodstoves
snowscape of lamplit cabins
inside by the fire
Phoenix the black cat snoozing on zafu
smoke rings in moonlight

pattern of every kimono
is code of abode- silent opera
echo of love affair
string music serenading stars
silky milk of comet's trail
tattooed by what's in your heart
aroma of skin t' skin
it wraps you in comfort
evaporates worry with wisdom
sewn by the in-out of breath
embroidered by season
thimble of ritual
patching when needed
those years off the grid
circular cabin full of toys-
that winter Kimono snowed & snowed
above windows we had t' dig our way
out the door t' replenish stove

Mike Parker

your thin fabric took the bite
from relentless winds
we three in love looking
out the window at driftmoods-

recall losing the path
asphalt music   i walked out
of Brownies Avenue A
at dawn wondering which way t' go-
first i had t' bury parents & friends
sweat on the loading docks
erode cannibal habits
& make my way back t' mountains
of poetry & kindling
switchbacking the need
t' document bearscat & ptarmigan
my marriage mapped an old trail
thru the watershed of a warm bed
& i found myself
on the slopes of hope above
treeline pipedreaming schemes
to sew a robe large enough
t' hold us three close-
once again when the fog
blew away there i was &
i wanted what i had
t' slip into something comfortable
& spend the night next t' you
trembling aspens whispering poems
kimono woven from the
essence of longing
t' linger in the moment
nature nurtured

Kimono Mountain

ephemeral phenomenon
serving up the tea of being-
i wanted what i had

kimono sometimes
evening front porch
streamside
barefoot in high tide
retreating in shade
unplugged without
scorch of headlines
thumbs touching each other
loss of smothering
return of why & how
kimono sometimes
footsteps in first snow
alone on the trail
dog walking in wildflowers
eyes up on meteor showers
ease found in breeze
humble on knees
off the clock
rock t' rock
detour restless for breathless
digging your way out of habit
snowshoeing thru rabbit prints-
from our first minutes
after our birth
it's warmth we seek-
slip into kimono
yawn in the mysteries
before we're gone gone
i'll never forget
i wanted what i had

Mike Parker

Feb 4   Night Meal

blood on the path
droplets from sharp teeth
running
    attacked at the chopping block
night meal of snowshoe hare
wind wiped hunger's tracks
of time's insatiable fable

Kimono Mountain

OxyMoron in the White House

the biggest crowd ever
the world needs ultimatums
mine is bigger than yours
spreading the wealth at the top
the bottom line i inherited a mess
tax time is for the poor
i actually won the popular vote
make this country late again
all options are under the table
the art of the deal is deceit
the U.S. will secede from America
raise your right hand and click your heels
Japan needs its own nuclear bomb
that guy in the Philippines might be right
what's wrong with walls look at China
i'm for affordable housing i build hotels
the intelligence agencies are dumb
reading is a waste of time i toilet twitter
i'm not bitter about the press
a black guy in the white house was scary
the top one percent need a brake
the two- state solution was overrated
didn't i tell you the truth
everybody loves coal
American prisons are the envy of the world
i'll fire the jobless
also mine is bigger than yours

Mike Parker

Parkerganda

that which tries
to contain the flow
is a sewer

ya gotta believe
in what ya know
is the right thing t' do-
vocal the awful
confront the wrathful
juice the joyful

weed between
the lies

pillow your worries
with the truth
you see in her eyes-
don't fear surprise

i love this town
we are the ethics
we breathe-
we tried
some died
some just went
t' seed

how i long t' be
the sound
of snow falling

Kimono Mountain

on these Indian Peaks
ah! ah! ah! ah! ah!

Mike Parker

August Hail

august hail bouncing off
my moss grown shoulders
monsoon mushrooms everywhere
six cords of oak in
propane in
pine for kindling coming
twisted steel roofing needs repair
ravens went crazy in the partial eclipse
brisk mornings, late berries

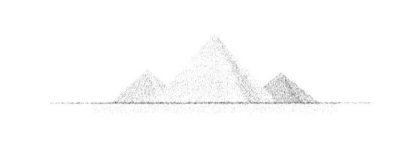

About The Author

Mike Parker was born in the brass mill town of Waterbury Connecticut in 1944. D'Spare Press published three collections of his poetry: *Don't Fall Off the Mountain, Wallflower Sutra*, and *Walking on Water in a Razorblade Breeze*, and he has three live poetry CDs. He sang in the band Ballistic Kisses, recording two albums on Beggars Banquet Records, *Total Access* and *Wet Moments*. He served two terms of Artist in Residence for the Ward Public Library and was the recipient of the Neodata Literary Fellowship from the Boulder County Arts Alliance. He lives with his wife the poet Mary Johnston Parker and daughter Frannie in the town of Ward Colorado on the edge of the Indian Peaks Wilderness.

Middle Creek Publishing Titles

Span
by David Anthony Martin

Deepening the Map
by David Anthony Martin

Phases
by Erika Moss Gordon

Cirque & Sky
by Kathleen Willard

Messiah Complex and Other Stories
by Michael Olin-Hitt

*Lessons from Fighting The Black Snake
at Standing Rock*
by Nick Jaina and Leslie Orihel

Wild Be
by One Leaf

Bijoux
by David Anthony Martin

Sawhorse
by Tony Burfield

Almost Everything, Almost Nothing
by KB Ballentine

Across the Light
by Bruce Owens

Kimono Mountain
by Mike Parker

ECO/CO Books is an imprint of Middle Creek Publishing & Audio dedicated to publishing All-Colorado books about the beautifully diverse Human Ecology of Colorado by Colorado authors and artists.

www.ingramcontent.com/pod-product-compliance
Lightning Source LLC
Chambersburg PA
CBHW070209100426
42743CB00013B/3115